THE CAT EMPIRE

The Secret Life of Merlin

Michael Weigall

CORGI BOOKS

THE CAT EMPIRE

A CORGI BOOK   0 552 99266 6

First publication in Great Britain

PRINTING HISTORY
Corgi edition published 1987

Copyright © Michael Weigall 1987

This book is set in 10/11pt Paladium.

Corgi Books are published by Transworld Publishers Ltd.,
61-63 Uxbridge Road, Ealing, London W5 5SA, in Australia
by Transworld Publishers (Australia) Pty. Ltd., 15-23 Helles
Avenue, Moorebank, NSW 2170, and in New Zealand by
Transworld Publishers (N.Z.) Ltd., Cnr. Moselle and
Waipareira Avenues, Henderson, Auckland.

Printed in Italy by A. Mondadori Editore - Verona

INTRODUCTION

T he star of the Cat Empire is a black and white alley cat called Merlin. His place and exact date of birth are not known to me for he was a stray who wandered one day into the house of friends who live in the west London suburb of Ealing.

His entry upon the scene in 1977 was a fitting prelude to a career that I hope will make him the most famous cat in the world. Soaked and emaciated, he appeared at my friends' kitchen window in the middle of a tremendous storm, his miaouing punctuated by rolls of Wagnerian thunder.

My friends knew I was looking for a feline companion. They always had several cats in residence and said I could choose whichever one I took a fancy to. I am a born ailurophile, the fancy name for people who love cats, from *ailuros*, the Greek for feline. The Bad Guys are called ailurophobes . . .

When I arrived I had no preconceived ideas. My love for cats was truly indivisible. I loved them all. I could not truthfully say the same of the people I had encountered in two successive careers, first in journalism, then as a film and television producer.

I had resolved to take home with me whichever cat purred for me. Merlin, who was busy chasing a butterfly in the garden, barely gave me a second glance as I surveyed the five cats on audition.

It seemed an *embarras de richesses*. As a true ailurophile, I found them all equally attractive. But Merlin was the only one who purred the moment I took him in my arms.

Merlin and I are now in our middle years together, but in a sense the Cat Empire was part of my life long before I met him.

As a small boy living first in Japan, where I was born, and later in France, I had strong recurring fantasies of a world inhabited only by cats. I spent hours designing passenger liners and warships manned by them.

The ships had cabins with cat-sized bunks. The cat navy had its own elaborate uniforms though, as yet, without mouse motifs. I loved animals, all animals, and in my child-like innocence, could not conceive that my much loved cats could harbour such antagonistic thoughts towards another species.

In this imaginary world, there was also a cat airforce, felines riding on saddles strapped on to seagulls that flew in perfect formation. There were cat train drivers, horse riders and priests and, of course, there was the King of the Cats. There was a cat national anthem that I hummed but, lacking a musical ear, I could never make the tune sound the same twice running.

To those who disapprove of giving human attributes to animals, I can quote only from my own experience: if you think of animals as people when you are a child, you grow up loving them more, not less.

My father was English and my mother French. My first cat recollection is of being made to dress up like one at a children's fancy dress party in Yokohama.

My mother had a brown velvet suit made for me with large triangular ears and a long brown tail that seemed as big as I was. Wearing it was a bit of an ordeal and my love for cats nearly suffered a blow from which it might never have recovered. On stage as the audience beamed, I made a few pitiful attempts to miaouw, then burst into tears!

But, as the Jesuits say, give us the child and we will create the man.

Concern for cats can make you stand out in a crowd sometimes. In Rome, where I worked as a Reuter correspondent, it once even had me assisting the carabinieri in their inquiries . . .

When it rained really hard, hundreds of the city's cat colony would be trapped by floodwaters on the marble monuments. With an English girl friend, I used to fill up a suitcase with hamburgers and toss them at the marooned cats.

Because of my French antecedents, I had been a hopeless cricket player at school, so many of the hamburgers fell short, to be lost with a splash in the swirling water, much to the cats' dismay.

A policeman mistook my mannah from heaven for an attempt to desecrate a state monument! Perhaps he even thought the hamburgers were hand grenades, not yet exploded. The day was saved only by producing my fortunately impressive-looking Ministry of the Interior press pass.

Merlin is the most vocal cat I have ever known. His wanderings around the house are set to a tuneful melody of varied croaks and miaous. Whether he is entering a room, leaping on or off a table or bed or simply returning a look, he has an appropriate sound to mark the event.

Back in 1869, a French writer about cats, Champfleury, counted 63 different types of miaous among cats of his acquaintance. Over the years feline experts have come up with a host of different tallies. But all of them seem to agree on one thing, that there really *is* a cat language.

As cats rarely miaou to each other, except on specific sexy occasions, it is obviously a language they have devised specially since the start of their voluntary domestication to pass on wishes or commands to their humans . . .

Merlin's deep purr — which I now know from the research for this book to be of the same frequency as an idling diesel engine, 25.9 cycles per second — has been the constant sound track on my years of happy relationship with him.

When I first experimented with dressing him up, I would not have continued had not his almost non-stop purring suggested he really was enjoying the attention.

Almost 30 starring roles later, I have to admit that the little gastronomic delicacies that make up his professional fee may also have had something to do with it . . .

Merlin is one hundred per cent a volunteer. People have told me how clever we were to superimpose his face on real people's photographs. But there is no superimposition. Merlin did actually sit in front of a photographic background or specially constructed set.

Merlin alone decided the length of each photo session. Sometimes he sat patiently through three or four rolls of film. But if he was bored, he would indicate that proceedings were at an end by tossing off his headgear with a quick shake of the head.

The only problem that ever arose with Merlin's costumes was if he forgot he was wearing one and tried to scratch. Sometimes I did the scratching for him!

Like humans, Merlin has fashion likes and dislikes. He enjoys soft hats, like Road Mog's cloth cap, but did not much take to dressing up as Senator Cato with his laurel wreath.

Merlin's minder and dresser at the photo sessions was an American lady, Carolyn Sweeny. Some of his earlier outfits, like the Maharajah's turban, came from her own exotic wardrobe. I am deeply indebted to her for her patience and skill and apologise for the teeth marks which were frequently to be observed in her fingers, the result of Merlin's over-eagerness to snatch his tit-bits!

I am also most grateful to Belinda Webster, a talented young graphic artist from New Zealand who became the set and prop maker to the Cat Empire. Whatever the décor, whether a giant Rat à l'Orange or a string of cat-sized onions for Monsieur Miaou, special care had to be taken to use only non-edible materials in case Merlin, a true universal gourmet, tried to tuck into the set!

Merlin's costumiers are Charles and Violet Batten, for whom being feline costumiers is an eccentric sideline to their main business of making hats for humans in Soho.

The Battens have never met Merlin. It was I who represented him at his costume fittings. But they knew his measurements exactly and the outfits rarely needed adjusting. I am greatly indebted to them, the more so since Violet Batten confessed to me on the day she delivered the last costume for this book, that she could not stand cats!

    I should also like to thank Max Morgan-Witts, Aury Shoa, Nigel
Turner and Camilla and Mark Ween Goldstein for supplying a background
from their travels; Chippy MacCloskey and Athena Gassoumis in New
York for making Merlin's flying and motoring goggles, and Jane Webster
and Roger Woddis for thinking up some good names!

    To Robyn, I am lovingly grateful, for her patient acceptance of our
drawing room being turned into a chaotic photographic studio for weeks
on end, and for not over-reacting when I used her piles of unique research
material to prop up the backgrounds or raise the velvet stool on which
Merlin sat for his photography . . .

    Last but not least, I am grateful to Diamond, Merlin's tabby companion
whom we love just as much, for not showing the jealousy he may perhaps
have felt at all the attention Merlin inevitably received on photography
days.

Michael Weigall
London, 1987.

W hen Merlin is excited by the rustle of the Sunday papers on the bed or chases a pingpong ball across the kitchen floor, he is responding to instincts all cats have had since prehistoric times, when early felines spied out and then chased the first rodents.

Merlin's most distant ancestor was a small, flesh-eating mammal called the miacis, who lived some 50 million years ago.

A bit like a modern weasel, it was a tenacious creature with a long body and short legs. It is the ancestor Merlin shares with bears, raccoons, hyenas and . . . dogs.

Three million years before Christ, man was still stumbling around, searching for his final shape. But the cat was already perfect. The way he looks today was laid down very early in evolution.

Forty different kinds of cats emerged from the Pleistocene era a million years ago, the time of the great Ice ages, when only the fittest and most adaptable forms of life survived, and all are still around today in a similar and recognisable form.

Cats preceded dogs by some ten to twenty million years, but the dog ended up getting himself domesticated long before the cat.

Cats obviously avoided having too close a contact with civilisation until it was advanced enough to keep them in the lap of luxury. History's first recorded case of domestication in cats is in the Egypt of the Pharaohs four millenia ago.

But some sort of domestication of the cat species may well have happened long before, when cavemen went out to kill a big cat and then took its cubs home as playthings for the cave children.

What saved the early cats from being clubbed and skinned like the other animals was the cavemen discovering that cats had a special knack for keeping rats out of the caves.

It was not long before the cat was sauntering on his silent pads into the story books.

According to an Arabian legend, there were no cats at first on the passenger list of Noah's Ark. The mice couple aboard decided to multiply and Noah, fearful the unexpected extra cargo might make his ship unseaworthy, called on the lion to help. The lion sneezed and, obligingly, two cats leapt from its nostrils. The mice were soon being kept in line.

MOGLODYTE

The world's oldest picture of a domesticated cat was found at Thebes on an Egyptian tomb of 4000 years ago. The feline, called Bouhabik, is probably history's first named cat.

The fertile valley of the Nile was the granary of the old world and the Egyptians founded a great religious cult around a cat goddess called Bastet that lasted for two thousand years.

In Ancient Egypt, cats were revered by pharaoh and peasant alike. House cats had their ears pierced to accommodate gold earrings and jewels. They were fed on bread and milk and slices of Nile fish and encouraged to eat from the same dish as their humans.

If a cat died, the whole family shaved off its eyebrows as a sign of mourning. If anyone killed a cat, even accidentally, the courts would sentence him to death.

Egypt's enemies cashed in on this, of course. In 525 B.C., the King of Persia was attacking the Egyptian city of Peluse. Knowing of his opponents' weakness for cats, he ordered each of his soldiers to carry one into battle. When the defenders saw that they could not repel the attack without hurting the cats, the city surrendered.

The export of cats was forbidden. The Egyptians knew when they were on to a good thing and wanted the cats to themselves.

The early Egyptians made use of the cat's hunting skills to help them in their own hunting. Cats leapt into the Nile to retrieve fowl slain by the hunters and were used to herd geese.

At the centre of the cult was Bastet's great temple at Bubastis, where sacred cats roamed freely. The job of caring for them was much sought after.

Every spring Bastet's statue was carried ceremoniously through the streets. Thousands of dancing fans converged on Bubastis, travelling on Nile barges that echoed to the music of flutes and castanets. By some accounts, the cat festivals were great human sex orgies too!

When cats died, they were sent to the temple to be mummified. As sustenance in the hereafter, mice also were mummified and placed in the tombs beside them, alongside saucers of milk.

Cats would never again be worshipped publicly on this scale although, of course, they still are in the privacy of millions of homes throughout the world.

PHARAOH FELIS

It was the Romans who spread the newly-domesticated cat across Europe.

The Romans first got interested in cats when they were illegally smuggled out of Egypt, in the knapsacks of Roman soldiers returning home.

One soldier, who killed a cat accidentally, was nearly lynched by an Egyptian mob in one of a series of incidents that led to the wars between Egypt and Rome.

When the cats arrived in Rome, they were employed as vermin controllers. The weasels and snakes hitherto used for this work soon found themselves redundant.

The Romans were impressed by the stories their soldiers told about the Egyptian cat cult and before long the cats were leading a life of luxury in Roman homes.

For the first time, cats found themselves being used in human medicine. Unhappily for them, it would not be the last. Pliny thought cats' faeces were medically beneficial. Mix them with mustard, he said, and they would cure ulcers in the human head.

Many domestic cats arrived in England aboard Roman galleys. But Merlin's ancestors may have arrived earlier still with the Phoenician traders who are credited with introducing the first domestic cat to England. They exchanged the cats for tin from Cornish mines!

Because the foreign cats bred with local wild cats, today's British moggy probably has some wild cat blood.

When the Roman armies spread across Europe, it was only natural that the cats should travel with them. Felines were emblazoned on the battle flags of several of Rome's legions.

Cats have not had only admirers in high Italian places. Julius Caesar could not stand them, nor, later, could Benito Mussolini.

But the feline connection was obviously important to the Romans. Witness the many towns they named after it, like Kattwyk ('Cats' Town') in the Netherlands or Caithness ('County of the Cats') in Scotland.

It is probably due to the advance of Rome's legions that the word for cat has a similar sound in all but one of Europe's languages . . . like *gatto* (Italian) . . . *chat* (French) . . . *gato* (Spanish) . . . *katze* (German) . . . *katti* (Finnish) . . . *kot* (Russian) . . . all probably derived from the Nubian word *kadis* picked up across the Mediterranean by the centurions who served in north-eastern Africa.

SENATOR CATO

'Teuton Tom' was Merlin's very first starring role.

As an indoor cat, Merlin had never needed to wear a collar. From my experience with cats earlier in my life, I knew they nearly always hated wearing one. But we were thinking of moving house and Merlin might have a garden to play in. A collar would be essential, an early trial probably helpful.

I had been given an old German Iron Cross. As a collar substitute, I tried it on Merlin, secured by its black, white and red silk ribbon.

I was expecting a dirty look. Instead Merlin started to chase Diamond around the flat, oblivious to the impediment dangling around his neck. He was still wearing it as he tucked into dinner that evening, indifferent to the clanking noises it made as it struck his plate.

It was a scene bizarrely reminiscent of a war film I had once seen. A German general, naked except for his Iron Cross, was dancing the night away at a way-out party in a castle near Prague. The cross jangled noisily against his partner's necklace, the only thing she was wearing too!

As a background for the Teuton Tom picture, I found an old German plaque in London's Portobello Road market. The plaque, from the pre-Nazi period, had once adorned a German consulate somewhere in Britain.

Merlin was suddenly on the road to stardom. It was on taking this photograph that I became aware for the first time of his incredible range of facial expressions.

An expert on animals as communicators had said cats had at least six easily readable expressions. But, as the Cat Empire developed, Merlin seemed to have a different one appropriate for each of his many roles.

For Tokyo Tiger and Peking Tom, he seems instinctively to assume an oriental countenance. As Americat, he has the reproachful look assumed by the Uncle Sam of the recruiting posters in the presence of anyone not wearing Marine Corps uniform! As Teuton Tom, on the other hand, his look is the glazed stare of a true fanatic at a Nuremberg rally.

TEUTON TOM

Merlin and I were both born in a Chinese Year of the Snake. It is a dubious credential. Prominent Snakes have included the composer Brahms, who used to shoot at cats with a bow and arrow, and Queen Elizabeth I, at whose coronation cats were put to death for the entertainment of the crowd.

Historically, cats have fared better in China, and indeed throughout Asia, than in Europe. Asian cats were not persecuted in the Middle Ages and life has always been relatively safe for them.

The Chinese were the first to note that the pupils of a cat's eye change shape according to the hour of the day, growing narrower until midday, when they are as thin as a hair, and wider again after noon. So, you can use a cat to tell the time!

The Chinese were also the first to observe that cats have psychic skills that enable them to predict danger, which is why they are, even now, featuring prominently in a Chinese earthquake warning scheme. 100,000 cat watchers are on permanent stand-by to monitor any strange behaviour by China's felines.

The Chinese word for a cat is pronounced 'mao', but cats were all the rage in China long before the eponymous Chairman.

In a Chinese legend, the cat is the result of mating a lioness with a monkey. The monkey made the cat playful and curious, while the lioness made it dignified and strong.

Such qualities made cats natural favourites at the court of the Ming emperors. One emperor went so far as to banish all dogs from court, replacing them with cats.

But felines had long been making their presence felt at the Chinese court. Along with many of her subjects, the Empress Wu of the earlier T'ang dynasty had embraced the old superstition that humans turned into cats when they died. She had one of her ladies-in-waiting executed. Just before her death, the hapless victim had threatened to turn her into a rat! The Empress decided to take no chances . . . She ordered the removal of *all* the palace cats.

In China, cats are credited with the ability to make the dead rise again. As this might, understandably, worry relatives hoping to inherit from a will, it is a tradition that felines are kept well away from any Chinese funeral!

PEKING TOM

The Japanese were late cat fanciers. It was not until the Tenth Century that they imported domesticated cats from China.

The jungle has almost disappeared on their crowded islands, but the cat is seen as a creature that can still bring the thrill of the wild into ordinary homes. That is why the house cat is known in Japan as 'the tiger that eats from your hand'.

At first cats were in short supply so only the nobility was allowed to have them. In Kyoto, the Imperial capital, noblemen liked to show off by parading their cats on silken leashes.

Japan's first recorded cat litter was born at the Imperial palace on 19th September 999. It was the Emperor Ichijo's 13th birthday and he gave orders for the kittens to be given the same care, food and clothes as the royal children.

In the Middle Ages cats became so popular as house pets in Japan that they gave up chasing rats and mice altogether. Rodents had such a field day, eating their way quickly through successive harvests, that in desperation a law was passed ordering all cats to be let loose and making it illegal to buy or sell one.

That is one of the reasons why ferocious looking felines are to be seen in so many old Japanese paintings. The Japanese hoped that, if real cats could not, wall illustrations of this kind might frighten off the rodents.

And the problem has not gone away. There have been reports of Japanese cats now actually being chased *by* rats! The Japanese blame the modern diet for their felines' shortcomings. Too much high protein meat has made them slothful. Too many cat naps, and lack of exercise generally, are giving them high blood pressure.

In spite of being failed mousers, Japan's cats still enjoy a popular image. The nation's folklore is filled with tales of cats who perform good deeds and whose presence brings luck.

In Tokyo an ailurophile can buy a tomb for his cat's ashes, with space alongside for his own urn so he can join him in due course.

If Japan's cats earn no plaudits nowadays for gallantry on the battlefield, their beauty has nonetheless inspired a long succession of Japanese artists skilled at adapting feline features to the oriental physiognomy.

TOKYO TIGER

Although cats are not mentioned in the Bible, religious artists began to feature them in later paintings of the Holy Family and, even in Catholic Italy, a legend arose that a cat had given birth to its kittens in Mary's stable at Bethlehem.

However, it has not always been clear on whose side the cat was supposed to be. In some portrayals of the Last Supper, a cat is shown crouching at the feet of Judas, with a distinct suggestion that he is about to rub himself purring against his legs!

When Christianity drove out the pagans, many of the qualities which the ancient Egyptians used to attribute to their cat goddess Bastet, like love for children and a concern for the sanctity of family, were all incorporated into the character of the Virgin Mary.

But, with cats associated with Christ's betrayal, it was perhaps inevitable that felines would play a negative role in Christianity for a long time to come.

However, since medieval times, cats have never been short of friends in ecclesiastical circles. At least three Popes, Leo XII, Gregory XV and Pius IX, were ardent admirers.

Leo XII reared Micetto, a large ginger and grey creature, on a fold of his white papal robe and gave him a free run of the Vatican's Sistine Chapel.

When Leo XII died, he willed Micetto to the French ambassador, Chateaubriand, another eminent ailurophile, who had convinced himself that he even looked like a cat. 'I think our long familiarity has given me some of his ways,' he liked to tell fellow diplomats.

An archbishop of Taranto astonished visitors by having his cats sit with him whenever he entertained in his palace at Naples. He told dinner guests 'You must pardon my passion for cats but you will find they make excellent company.'

A true cat lover does not need much convincing that cats have souls. The French writer Théophile Gautier, observed of his cat's familiar habit of staring at him with unblinking eyes: 'They almost frighten you, for it is impossible to believe that a soul is not there.'

Carl van Vechten, author of *The Tiger in the House*, one of our century's great classics about felines, was quite sure that 'a Heaven without cats would be deserted for a Hell with them.'

MAGNIFICAT

It was in the Middle Ages, when witches took over from wizards as the main purveyors of magic, that cats became associated in the public mind with sorcery.

In the Middle Ages cats had a higher legal status than they do today, but it was used to persecute them, not protect them. They were thought moral agents and so could be sued or tried.

For many a lone woman, it was enough to be old and ugly and to have a black cat as a pet, to be accused of being a witch.

An estimated ten million women throughout Europe whose only crime it was to keep a cat, were convicted of witchcraft and put to death. Millions of cats were sent with them to the stake.

It was a hard time for cats in general. They were gaily tossed into the flames at religious festivals. Many towns celebrated a Holy Day by throwing felines from the church belfry.

Cats were under attack even for the way their eyes shone at night! Of the perils of meeting one in the dark, Edward Topsell said in his *Historie of Four-Footed Beastes* published in 1607 'When a man commeth to see a cat on the sudden and in the night, they can hardly be endured for their flaming aspect.'

Certainly nothing even remotely similar to the persecution of the cat happened in the story of the dog. It was the way cats kept their independence that infuriated so many people. When the witch hunting began, it was easy to accuse cats of being anti-social.

There is a footnote to this unhappy period. When the Plague swept medieval Europe, cats had the last word. It spread so quickly because rats were the carriers, and the witch hunters had seen to it there were no longer enough cats around to keep them in check.

MAGICAT

Merlin is not very keen on French cooking as he considers it too spicy, although he is partial to French cat food which we buy for him on occasional trips across the Channel.

Having spent my own childhood in France, I remember how popular cat stories were among schoolchildren. A really spooky one, which excited us all, concerned the Count of Comburg's wooden leg which stomped around on its own in a haunted castle, accompanied only by a huge black cat.

The French think of themselves as liberty's natural custodians. It was obvious therefore that they would regard the cat as a like-minded creature. The First French Republic featured a feline no less than twice on its coat of arms.

After the cat's persecution in the Middle Ages, it was the French who paved the way for his rehabilitation. In Louis XV's reign, cats swarmed all over the royal palace at Versailles. Medals were struck to honour them and their mysterious qualities were enthused over endlessly in Paris salons.

Cardinal Richelieu, the statesman, so adored cats that he left his fourteen felines and their minders a substantial legacy. He liked to be escorted by a posse of cats as he moved about on his affairs of state.

Merlin, whose greediness knows no bounds, would have liked the bit about Richelieu having special dining rooms for his cats where junior clerics fed them chicken pâté twice a day.

The cat's philosophic detachment has given him many admirers among French writers and artists.

The poet Baudelaire found them as captivating as women. Théophile Gautier, the writer, loved to be portrayed painted in a Turkish costume with a feline harem swarming all around him.

In a bizarre episode last century, King Louis Philippe ordered his Interior Ministry to pay a scientist 50,000 francs to write a book proving that, anatomically at least, it was the cat who was king of the creation!

But French cats have not only had friends in high places. They reached them too, French felines twice being sent into space. In the 18th Century the astonomer, Joseph Lalande, added *Felis*, a 'cat' star, to the astronomical map. 'I adore cats and may be forgiven for putting one in the sky,' he explained. In 1963 his successors did it for real, sending a reluctant cat called Felix 163 miles into the sky over the Sahara desert aboard a Véronique rocket.

MONSIEUR MIAOU

The cat has been a creature of mystery since all those ailurophiles in ancient Egypt first placed him on a pedestal 40 centuries ago. Yet, busybodies that they are, scientists all over the world are donning their white coats to try and unravel his secrets.

At the Max Planck Institute, a scientific research empire with headquarters in Bavaria, they have even been studying the cat to discover why it purrs.

The same cat may feel equally at home in the smartest salon and on the grimiest rooftop, but that is not to say that cats are the standard bearers for a classless society. For the way they purr is apparently one of their ways of showing their social position in the cat world.

According to the Germans, cats are capable of imitating the purr of other cats if it will help them gain entry into a different feline circle.

A pedigreed cat normally purrs in a way that sets him apart from the lesser cats but he might mimic their purr to show he is not stuck up. Similarly, an ordinary moggy may imitate the purr of his betters if he is engaging in a bout of social, as opposed to rooftop, climbing!

Cats first had a chance to show off their skill at purring in public over a century ago when the world's first cat show was held at London's Crystal Palace in 1871.

The existence of the millions of struggling proletarian cats outside was acknowledged by a special prize for 'workingmen's cats.'

The shows were intended to promote love and admiration for cats among the general public, but they were really great society occasions, a feline version of the debutantes' ball. Titled ladies in large numbers would converge on London and other show cities with a retinue of up to a dozen haughty cats and as many servants.

Although cats are not too much in favour in royal circles nowadays — Buckingham Palace is clearly one place where dogs hold sway — things were different then. At one show, King Edward VII even offered a signed photograph of himself to the winning cat.

The organisers feared unworthy cats might try to trick their way in with their imitation purrs. Yet the rules were surprisingly lax in those early days: a competitor was allowed to bite the judge three times before being disqualified!

BIERKELLER KAT

Cats have yet to learn to cope with one aspect of their environment, the motor car.

The underneath of a car provides a shelter for urban cats living out of doors, as they do in very large numbers in cities such as Rome. Cats know that none but the most determined human crawler can get at them in that confined space.

But the car is also the biggest feline killer. More cats die from road accidents in the developed countries than from any other cause, apart from old age. More males than females die on the roads, presumably because toms have a greater wanderlust.

Statistically, it is black and white cats who are most likely to be run over, presumably because there are more of them and they are harder to see. Happily, the closest Merlin comes to the automobile age is when, from the safety of his window shelf, he surveys nightly the traffic in our square for signs of my return home.

Cats have one of the most acute hearings in the animal kingdom — They can recognise their humans' footsteps several hundred feet away and tell the difference between one car engine and another.

As I approach our home in my car, I can sometimes see Merlin perk up visibly on his perch on the third floor. As soon as I have parked and disembarked, he vanishes from the window and runs to take up position at the front door for his ritual welcoming leap on to my shoulder.

The car is also behind the strange story of the British bionic cat. Tigger, a moggy in Brighton, had his right leg rebuilt with metal parts after an encounter with an automobile. Skin and fur were grafted over the injured limb so he looked exactly like an ordinary cat, except that he made a clanking sound if he struck anything! In spite of his handicap, Tigger had one consolation: The knowledge that any dog who tried to bite him would need urgently to consult a dentist!

ROAD MOG

I n Merlin's fantasies of the wild, the aeroplane must seem like a great pterodactyl, sent to taunt him.

Our home is on one of the approach routes taken by the helicopters which transport the Prince and Princess of Wales to and from Kensington Palace. From their window, Merlin and Diamond always crane excitedly for a better view of the flying monster. On a sunny day, they will chase its shadow across the floor.

Although I am sure he is not aware of it, Prince Charles once brought a modelling session to an abrupt end. As his helicopter passed overhead, Merlin leapt off his velvet modelling stool and sprinted to the window, leaving a costume trail and his discarded headgear rolling crazily across the floor.

Lone aviators have found cats make excellent companions to be cooped up with in a cockpit. An American ace of the First World War, Theodor Hammeker, always flew with his cat Brutus in his draughty open cockpit. Charles Lindberg, on the other hand, left his black cat behind when he crossed the Atlantic, because he did not want to risk the cat's life along with his own.

Cats have always had an ambiguous relationship with flying objects. The way birds move makes them potentially as exciting as mice. But even cats living out in the wild get only a quarter of their nutrition from eating birds.

This is not because of some gastronomic allergy. Birds are relatively safe from leaping cats — they have a ninety per cent chance of surviving an assault — because cats are not too good at controlling their speed or aim when their feet are off the ground.

If Merlin's interest flagged during a photographic session, I sometimes played him a tape of buzzing flies. The guaranteed result was a look of rapt attention! Real flies entering the air space of our home have a virtually zero life expectancy. Merlin regards them as a great delicacy.

FLYING TIGER

Merlin's consuming passion is food. His modelling fee is paid in his favourite currency, tiny morsels of the choicest turkey or ham offered during the photo sessions.

Merlin is so greedy that he is able to wake instantly from the deepest catnap, if he thinks he hears someone stealthily opening the refrigerator door on the floor below. In only a few seconds he is charging down the stairs to stake his claim!

Merlin is an exceptionally fast eater — does it stem from his early days as a stray, when food was hard to find? — and Diamond, his companion, a slow one. They eat on separate plates. A certain amount of policing is needed to make sure that Merlin does not elbow Diamond out of the way to finish off his food for him.

A cat has thirty teeth, only two fewer than a human, and the largest eyes of any mammal in relation to body size. In Merlin's case, it is undoubtedly the better to spy out edibles wherever they are to be found.

Weight for weight, a cat needs about a third more calories than its human. The average cat eats about 350 kilocalories of animal protein each day, which is twice as much as the average African. In a year a cat will eat twenty times its own weight in food, the equivalent of a human eating ten pounds of food every day of the year!

In the search to please the feline palate, there are even books on gourmet cat cuisine with complex recipes for such delicacies as 'O Sole Miaou'.

Cats are choosy about what they eat and get bored easily. For the cat food manufacturer, it is a struggle to find enough variety. But the one who hit on the idea of grinding down mice and putting them in cans got the thumbs down. His customers obviously did not think much of a mouse snack served without the thrill of the chase!

CATERER

Plats du Jour
Raton à l'Orange
Ratatouille Provençale
Fricadelles de Souris
à la Niçoise

Suprêmes de Raton
Archiduc

Salade de Catnip.

From Mesopotamia to Mexico, mousing is the one instinct all cats are supposed to have in common, but Merlin is an exception.

The first time I saw him confront a real mouse, he did not know what to do and hid under the bed for safety, leaving it to Diamond to deal with.

When the mouse appeared in the middle of the night, there were strange scuffling sounds and I found Merlin quivering with anxiety. For Diamond, who inevitably suffers a bit from Merlin's stardom, it was a rare chance to pull one over on his senior companion.

Cats hunt rodents for sport, not food, and it is courage, not under-feeding by its human, that turns a cat into a good mouser. An experiment held in Germany, to see how many mice a cat could comfortably kill off at one sitting, revealed an average of fifteen.

Humans did not domesticate the cat. Rather, they moved in on us when they found that the granaries built by the early farmers housed mice and rats as well as grain.

Humans quickly found they could not do without cats. Frederick the Great in 18th Century Germany thought so highly of those guarding his army's food stores that he gave them all honorary military ranks. He made each town he conquered provide him with a levy of cats, so he would always have a fresh supply of guards for his granaries.

In this period, a new kind of rodent, the brown rat, was taking over from the black rat, of Plague notoriety. The brown rat was cleverer, more versatile, even more dangerous.

But this time the line would hold. Cats were taken on everywhere as the buttress against the new menace. After all the setbacks of previous centuries, the cat was confirmed for the first time as a legitimate member of society, and accepted on his own terms.

The history of civilisation might have been different but for cats. Without them to keep rodents at bay, life would have been untenable in ancient Egypt and might even be so in our modern cities.

MEXICO MOUSER

U nlike dogs, cats have far too much independence of spirit ever to be dragooned into anyone's army as regimental mascots. Nonetheless, their skills have been sought after by the generals.

It was way back in 1535 that the military first tried to enlist cats into military service. An Austrian artilleryman devised a plan to strap tubes containing poisonous vapours to the backs of cats, then let the felines loose in enemy lines! Curiously, the scheme never won favour with the generals and the enemy went on breathing happily, but the blueprint is still on view at the city library in Strasbourg.

During the First World War, the British government advertised for 'Common Cats — any numbers' and half a million were recruited. Some served aboard submarines, their sensitive nostrils attuned to give early warnings of foul air, while others were introduced into the trenches to alert the soldiers to gas attacks.

During the Second World War, at the Battle of Stalingrad, a Russian cat called Mourka made headlines around the world by darting to and from across the battlefield with vital messages about German gun emplacements.

In the London Blitz, felines used their psychic ability to sense danger to warn their humans of impending air attacks. Minutes before the sirens sounded, cats were suddenly interrupting their meals and making their way, miaouing, towards the air raid shelters.

At the height of the war, Winston Churchill always insisted that his cat Nelson join him at meals and an official would be dispatched to find the cat so the meal could begin. Adolf Hitler, it almost goes without saying, was an out-and-out ailurophobe!

Military cats even served in Vietnam. Because a cat's eyesight is more sensitive than a human's, the Pentagon thought the felines could help U.S. troops on night patrol find their target.

Specially trained cats were flown secretly to Vietnam for evaluation trials in the jungle. But the project ended in fiasco when the cats led the heavily-armed patrols to mice rather than Vietcong hideouts!

EL GENERAL GATO

By all accounts, cats are as good at following a trail as the best Red Indian warrior.

Not a week passes without the newspapers chronicling yet another amazing tale of a feline's journey over a barely believable distance.

Naturally ailurophobes have heaped scorn on the notion that cats actually might have a noble motive for returning to a familiar place.

The 18th Century French naturalist, Georges Louis Leclerc, Count of Buffon, sneered that if cats really did make these long trips, it was simply because they were lazy; that they just could not face the thought of having to get to know a new home and its mouseholes. That was why, he claimed, they always tried to make it back to the place where they already knew the mice's hiding-places.

The cat's ability to navigate successfully without visual clues has been much investigated and an astounding number of claims have been authenticated.

Wisconsin scientists took cats out in rowing boats going round in circles to see if they could be disorientated by the nautical merry-go-round. But, sure as fate, the cats kept moving to the side of the boat which pointed towards their homes on terra firma!

In northern Germany, scientists took a large number of cats various distances from their homes and then turned them loose at the centre of a specially designed maze, with 24 exits pointing in all directions. In less than an hour, most of the cats had headed unerringly to the one closest to their home.

A popular explanation for this is that cats may be unusually sensitive to the earth's geomagnetic pull, thus enabling themselves to get a feline version of a compass fix on their home.

But none of this explains some cat's ability to find absent owners in a faraway place to which they have never before been.

One such journey took a cat called Sugar half-way across the United States, a fourteen-month trek over 1500 miles, to rejoin a family who had given him away when they moved from Anderson in California to Gage in Oklahoma.

CHIEF SITTING CAT

Cats, unlike some famous sailors — it is said that Admiral Horatio Nelson was not only often seasick but could not swim either — are excellent swimmers. Nonetheless, they hate water and will not enter it willingly.

Merlin has twice fallen into the bath while trying to catch a mechanical swimming frog I bought him one Christmas. He seemed to regard it more as an affront to his dignity than an experience akin to being a ship's cat aboard the *Titanic*.

Cats feature in many sailors' superstitions and it is not surprising that so many nautical terms have a cat connotation. *The International Maritime Dictionary* lists no fewer than twenty-two. Merlin would not be the only one aboard who knew what the captain was on about if there was a shout of 'Get to the cat-head and look lively on the cat back!'

If however the crew observed that he had 'a gale of wind in his tail,' it might be wiser to seek an alternative means of transport, as this is a reference to the sailor's belief that when a ship's cat is more playful than usual, the ship will soon sail into a storm.

The ever-cautious Japanese take no chances, sailing whenever they can with a tortoiseshell cat 'to keep the demons at bay'.

Until the 18th Century, French ships had by law to carry a cat on board to keep rodents in check. Even today insurance companies in some countries will not meet a claim for cargo nibbled away by rats if they can prove there was no ship's cat.

Cats get attached to their ships. Before the Second World War, departing ships had a number of ritual whistles. The half-hour whistle was the one recalling the crew aboard. The last, five minutes before departure, was the 'cat's whistle'. With their finely tuned hearing, many a ship's cat had become dependent on this toot for making it back on time. When it was discontinued during the war, many ship's felines were stranded in strange ports!

CAT O' NINE TAILS

In the early days in Australia, cats wandering ashore from the explorers' ships had to mate with each other as there were no sexy locals waiting on the quayside.

For Australia, in spite of its great outdoors, is one of the tiny handful of places in the world — along with New Zealand, Madagascar and a few Oceanic islands — where the cat is not indigenous.

Cats of one kind or another are to be found in every other part of the world. The cobbers are a zoological oddity because of the great land bridge that in primeval times connected Australia to south-east Asia.

South-east Asia eventually developed more different cat species than anywhere else in the world, but when the felines first arrived there, it was too late to make it across the land bridge as Australia had already broken away from Asia.

When a new civilization drops anchor, the cat has always been one of the first to go ashore. Enrolling as a ship's cat was not simply a way for felines to see the world. In those early days it was the only way in which cats could meet and cross-breed with other cat species in isolated parts of the world.

You can study human migratory patterns over the centuries simply by looking at the way cats' markings have been distributed around the world!

The early cobber cat must have welcomed the chance of a new life on a continent where felines, lacking a past, were judged solely on personality and performance. They quickly felt at home when they discovered the human locals also possessed a quite feline-like independence of spirit.

Cats have thrived in Australia in spite of their unorthodox start. Cobber cats have nudged at world feline records. A Sydney mouser recently weighed in at three stones three pounds and ten ounces!

And Australian cats are doing their best to populate the remainder of those open spaces, a Siamese Blue Point having produced one of the biggest litters ever recorded. She had thirteen little Australian kittens, about three times the world average.

CORKER CAT

Heroes in early Egypt, cats were to be in favour once more in the Arab world. For the founder of the Moslem religion, the Prophet Mahommet, was a great ailurophile.

In Mahommet's time, the goings-on in ancient Egypt were already part of distant history and the cat was not well known in Arabia. One day, in a gesture which millions of cat lovers will understand, Mahommet wanting to respond to the priest calling the faithful to prayer, found his little cat Muezza asleep on the sleeve of his robe. Rather than disturb him, he promptly cut off the sleeve so Muezza could continue his catnap!

The cat may not be mentioned in the Bible, but it is, several times, in the Koran. Thanks to Mahommet, the cat remained for a while the favourite animal of Moslems.

At a time when cats in their millions were being massacred in Europe, a sultan in 13th Century Cairo was the first person in the world to leave a legacy for strays. He left the income from his substantial fruit orchards to provide food for the city's cats at prayer time.

Each day, for many centuries to come, hundreds of cats gathered to tuck in ravenously the moment they heard the muezzin's call from the minaret. Successive owners of the orchards honoured the legacy until recent times.

The Middle East is one part of the world where cats should feel really at home. For a start, they share with the camel the rare and curious habit of moving their fore and hind legs at the same time.

Being much less sensitive to extremes of temperature than their humans, felines also love the great heat. The feline body instinctively responds to heat changes and German scientists have even claimed that you can tell a room's temperature simply by observing how a cat is sleeping. They found cats have 400 different sleep positions, all dependent on the ambient temperature!

In the Middle Ages, people buying a cat always looked for scorch marks on its fur. If there were any, it meant the cat had spent too much time lounging near a fire, so it could not possibly be a good mouser!

PURRAMID CAT

One superstition about felines was shared widely among the peoples of the East, the belief that after death the human soul can live on inside a cat.

Visitors to Poona in the last century were amazed to see the Hindu sentries at Government House presenting arms to every feline, even battle-scarred old toms, that passed through the portals.

Ailurophiles would see that as nothing more than a just tribute to the true king of the animals, but the Hindu men-at-arms were not cat lovers, simply superstitious.

What had happened was that the Governor of Bombay, Sir Robert Grant, had died there and, on the night of his demise, a cat was observed scurrying from the building. The cat went along the same path the Governor used to take his nightly 'constitutional'.

A priest talked in the barracks about the transmigration of the soul — how it could switch from one body to another — and the soldiers became convinced the Governor's soul had passed into one of the household's pets! The problem was no one knew which one, so it was decided the sentries should salute *all* the cats. Incredibly, this remained a standing order for a quarter of a century.

Cats in substantial numbers appeared relatively late on the Indian scene, in the second century before Christ, a testimonial to how well the Egyptian embargo on cat exports was working!

In Europe, the religious frenzy aroused during the witch hunts of the Middle Ages was soon left far behind. But on the Indian sub-continent, as recently as the 1960s, a cat in high places showed that felines were still able to trigger powerful emotions when religion was at stake.

A row which involved the United States and Pakistan governments, blew up over the name the American ambassador in Delhi had chosen for his pet cat. The diplomatic moggy was called Ahmed and, as devout Moslems, the Pakistanis were hopping mad because Ahmed is one of the various names by which Moslems knew their Prophet.

In the Pakistan parliament, the Deputy Speaker proclaimed it was a worse insult than all the American military aid to India. The Americans quickly changed the cat's name!

Somehow it all seemed a far cry from the days of Mahommet, the great ailurophile.

MAHARAJAH OF KATPUR

P erhaps it is because of their own love of freedom that cats have shown such sympathy for imprisoned humans! Early in the 17th Century a black and white moggy very much like Merlin found himself at the grim walls of Britain's oldest fortress, the Tower of London.

The cat had managed to track down his human, Henry Wriothesley, the third Earl of Southampton, who was imprisoned at the Tower for suspected treason. After a hazardous journey across the labyrinth of defences, the cat climbed down a chimney, finally to appear in the prison chamber for an emotional reunion with his human.

Another famous prisoner, Sir Henry Wyat, gaoled by King Richard III in the 15th Century, received several clandestine visits from his feline, who brought him pigeons to supplement the prison fare!

Britain can claim what may be the world's earliest reference to cats in a legal document. A Welsh law of the 10th Century codified a cat's value. Until its eyes opened, a kitten was worth one penny. But later, as a practised mouser, the cat would be worth four pennies, more than a Welsh lamb!

In Queen Victoria's time, London and other British cities were thronged with working cats. After centuries of ill treatment, cats again enjoyed a privileged legal situation. The law protected them against being beaten, long before the same protection was extended to children.

Cats were introduced into the British Post Offices in 1868 to stop rats from helping themselves to the Royal Mail. Postmasters all over Britain had to file *weekly* reports on the felines' efficiency. Cats have been on the Post Office pay roll ever since.

One department of state, the Home Office, has been guarded for a century by a succession of salaried mousers, all of them called Peter. Even today, the British government employs 100,000 cats to keep its property safe from rodents.

But Queen Victoria herself would not join in the general euphoric belief that cats alone could cope with the problem. She had an official Rat Catcher at court, a human in a gaudy uniform festooned with rat insignias and a VR emblem. The Queen must have thought that cats were getting soft!

YEOMAN MOUSER

When cats became available in America in large numbers in the middle of the 18th century, it was like the arrival of the Seventh Cavalry.

For rodents were already circling the waggons. Forty rodent groups with 750 sub-varieties were busy destroying the crops as fast as the settlers could plant them.

Now the American cat is the world's most pampered feline. Cats there are neck-and-neck with dogs in the popularity stakes. America has an estimated 50 million domestic cats, twice as many as in the early 1970s. They live in some 25 million homes, so after pioneering the two-car family, the United States has achieved the two-cat home!

The felines are courted by a burgeoning industry. There are special cat mail order houses and, as the American cat is now largely an indoor pet, there are pages of appropriate advertisements ranging from a self-cleaning litter box called the 'Kitty Kastle' to devices that enable cats to use their humans' lavatories. A wide range of 'Fancy Furniture For Furry Friends' includes antique-style decorated screens so a cat may have privacy on his box.

There is a Mewspaper publishing company and an 11-year-old American cat called Lincoln has become the world's first feline to be implanted with a pacemaker.

For humans unable to bear the thought of bereavement, there are schemes to preserve your cat intact, ancient Egyptian-style, by a freeze-drying process.

As elsewhere, American cats are under attack for not chasing after rats with enough enthusiasm. In Massachusets, disconcerted investigators found cats and rats living happily alongside each other in half of the State's farms!

One canine redoubt has so far managed to hold the feline assault troops at bay . . . the White House. With very few exceptions, America's Presidents have liked to be associated publicly with dogs, presumably because of the latter's more macho image.

One of America's great ailurophiles was Mark Twain, who lived with 19 cats near Elmira, New York. 'If a man could be crossed with a cat,' he predicted confidently, 'it would improve the man but deteriorate the cat.'

AMERICAT

In a real life Cat Empire, it is the cat's rival, the dog, who would be a socialist. Dogs' ancestors used to roam around in packs, each with a leader. So, when dogs were domesticated, it was easy for them to switch their allegiance to a human master.

The cat, an anarchist at heart, belongs to an earlier period of Russian history when defiance of authority was all the rage! Felines have never been under anyone's yoke.

In spite of attitudes which would make them dissidents in modern Russia, cats delighted Lenin and the composer Rimsky Korsakov, giving an account of a dinner party he attended given by a fellow composer, Borodin, related how several cats paraded across the table, sticking their noses into plates and leaping without further ceremony onto the guests' backs, much to the host's obvious delight!

But it has not been laughter all the way in the workers' paradise. Stalin ate cat frequently during his exile in Siberia.

Cat superstitions abound throughout Eastern Europe. When a cat is put out in a thunderstorm, it is because of an old belief among Slavs that this is the precise moment when 'devils enter a cat's body.' Lightning is said to be thrown down by angels trying to drive the devils out. If the cat was allowed to stay indoors, the lightning might accidentally set the house on fire.

In Bulgaria, in the mountain town of Gabrovo, the regular venue for a 'World Laughter Festival', there is a strange cat legend which ailurophiles might find a bit short on hilarity! The town's mascot is a cat without a tail. Not because he was born that way but because, so legend has it, the Gabrovians, known throughout the Balkans for their thrift, used to cut the tail off. The idea was that by shortening the length of the cat's body, it would not keep the door open so long in winter-time, thus saving fuel costs.

MOSCOW MOGGY

Back in the 17th Century, Miguel Cervantes, author of *Don Quixote*, wrote about a Spanish prince called Timonel of Carcarjona whose shield showed a golden cat and the word 'Miau' as a tribute to his beautiful wife Miaulina.

Admittedly, few ailurophiles have felt it necessary to affirm their love of felines publicly by adopting a cat-sounding name themselves. But if anyone deserves a cat name, it must surely be a lady. Many people find it genuinely easier to refer to a cat, even a battling tom, as 'she'.

The association between felines and the human female is as old as the domestication of the cat. It was no accident that ancient Egyptians picked a cat *goddess* to be the cult figure in their life.

Women and felines have suffered equally in history because of the oriental notion, dreamed up at a time when all men were male chauvinists, that of all the animal species, the cat was the closest to woman. This was not just because of its suppleness and the voluptuous curves which have delighted artists over the ages, but because of its personality.

One explanation for today's undoubted revival of cats' popularity has been to link it with the success of the women's liberation movement. Cats are seen as the natural beneficiaries of the decline in the macho image supposedly represented by dogs.

Certainly you can detect male chauvinists at work behind much ailurophobia. When women are accused of being 'catty', it is because they are 'cruel', 'sly', 'fickle', 'deceitful', 'ungrateful', 'emotionally inconstant' . . . the very reputation ailurophobes have been trying to unload on cats for centuries! When American men go off in search of illicit sex, where should they head for but the cat-house!

In ancient Egypt, women made up their eyes to look like felines'. Cats were looked upon as symbols of happiness and fertility as well as shrewdness and resourcefulness. But, as always, there was a darker side to the connection. When an adulterous woman was sentenced to die and thrown into the Nile, a cat was always tossed in with her.

CATALONIAN

Cats are always ready to jump into bed.

In fact, Merlin, along with most other felines, spends two thirds of his time asleep, taking cat naps. In a lifetime of, say, fifteen years, a cat will have spent only five of those years awake!

Tom cats are sexually mature when they are about one. Merlin came into my life as a stray when he was still very young. He had been neutered in his earlier life, so it is unlikely he ever took part in any sexual frolics. I know Diamond has not.

As Merlin and Diamond sit on their window shelf listening to the caterwauling in the square below, I feel bad about that. But there is the selfish consolation of knowing that a neutered cat's life expectancy is about twice that of an active tom.

Being so independent, a cat likes to find his own place to sleep, but it does not stop his humans from spending a small fortune trying to lure him into a kitty bed! Cat magazines have page after page of advertisements for aids to catnapping. There's the 'ultimate cat house' and beds of all kinds from rustic to brass, with pillows to match, even enhance, the humans' decor.

There is a multitude of strangely-shaped scratching-posts, some looking like obstacles in an army assault course, and there are cat water beds. If a cat exercised his claws as often as Merlin and, still dozy from a catnap, were to mistake one for the other, the result could be quite alarming!

Back in the 13th Century Bartolomeus Anglicus described the cat as a 'full lecherous beast' who was always 'swyft, plyant and merry . . .'

For any modern cats who might find it hard to live up to that exacting description, the American *Cat Fancy*, the world's largest circulation feline magazine, has a regular column called 'Cats On The Couch', which is crammed with advice for maladjusted felines from a psychoanalyst.

Cats are discreet lovers. Unlike a dog who will flaunt his love for every passer-by to see, a cat keeps his sex life to himself. His boudoir will be out of sight, tucked away in some bush or dark alley, even if his love song — the noises-off from the square which so perplex Merlin and Diamond on their window perch — can sometimes be mistaken for the screech of a dying heroine in an Italian opera!

PURRFECT PARTNER

As cats go out to seek their nightly pleasures, they wander into a world where ailurophobes have been lying in wait for centuries.

Over the years most countries have passed a multitude of laws trying to make cats behave in a way acceptable to humans.

The world's first legal document on cats, the Welsh statute in the 10th Century, was even an early example of consumer protection: it made anyone selling a cat 'responsible for it not caterwauling every moon'!

Legislators in America have, at one time or another, tried to impose every manner of restriction on cats, even curfews like the ones imposed after civil disorders, or forcing humans to keep them on a leash, which must surely be the ultimate indignity for an animal which has resisted domestication, other than on its own terms, for 40 centuries.

Cats have been making their presence felt in the world's courtrooms for ages. Back in 1540, a French bishop tried to excommunicate all the local mice as punishment for devouring that year's crop.

The mice were summoned to appear before him. When none showed up, a lawyer successfully argued that cats were to blame for his clients' non-appearance and the case was dropped!

Cats, unlike dogs, are still not regarded as property in the eyes of the law in most countries. It means they cannot be sued for trespass, but even this civil right has had to be fiercely fought over.

As early as 1624, a judge ruled that no human could reasonably be expected to confine a cat to his own property. But it was not much of a victory. If a cat wandered too far from home in those days, something terrible was likely to happen to him anyway.

More recently, Illinois was the scene of a dramatic action replay when Adlai Stevenson was State Governor. A coalition of dog and bird interests had managed to get a bill passed by the State legislature, imposing fines on anyone who allowed their cat to run at large. Vetoing the bill, Mr Stevenson said in a historic judgment that it was 'in the nature of cats to do a certain amount of unescorted roaming.'

TOP CAT IN LAS VEGAS

Merlin does not know too many dogs but he resembles his large relative, the tiger, much more closely than in the dog world a Pekinese does a Dalmatian. Cats have looked the same since prehistoric times but it can be difficult to postively identify certain breeds of dog!

In spite of the difficulties, there has never been a shortage of applicants for the post of Dog Catcher. In some parts of America they are even elected!

There are no official Cat Catchers, but unhappily, history has shown there are many other ways to snare a cat.

Ailurophiles like to think the cat is a better philosopher and judge of character. A dog may be taken in by soft-sounding words, but a cat will see through a kindly manner that is not genuine. Merlin can spot an ailurophobe in sheep's clothing a mile off.

Cats like to think they are smarter. Comparatively, even a kitten's brain is larger than a child's. In tests, cats have demonstrated they have a memory which is up to 200 times more retentive than that of a dog.

So perhaps cats at least can remember when cat and dog were friends. Could it be that their 'enmity' is not hereditary but created by man when the two species became rivals for our love as household companions?

Millions of cats and dogs coexist peacefully. Certainly, animal literature is filled with accounts of their love for each other . . . dogs rescuing drowning kittens . . . cats leading rescue teams to dogs buried in the rubble of British cities during the Blitz.

Cats have long known they are perfect, although it has taken us humans a long time to appreciate this. Now, in virtually every developed country cats are creeping up on dogs in popularity.

Cats know they make easier companions and are better suited to town living. They do not need to go on long walks. They do not bark. They leave no piles of excrement on the pavement. They do not grow to a huge size.

In a survey of veterinary surgeons carried out in the United States, none had even heard of an inebriated cat, but nearly all had drunken dog patients . . .

Dogs may well be taking to the bottle as they realise who is now 'top dog'!

HOT PUSSUIT

Since he first strode into recorded history 4000 years ago the cat has been alternately venerated and feared, persecuted and petted. He has been vilified as the devil's accessory, revered as a god . . . He has been used as a weather vane, a time piece and a thermometer . . . He has served in submarines, the Post Office and Vietnam . . . He has been the confidant of Popes and of Mahommet . . . He is the boss in millions of ordinary homes.

It is hard to have equivocal feelings about felines. They have always aroused strong emotions.

In the 17th Century Edward Topsell said of the ailurophobes' plight upon encountering a cat: 'they fall into passions, frettings, sweatings, pulling off their hats and trembling fearfully.'

A French king, Henry III, always fainted when a cat walked in. Napoleon was once found, panic-stricken, half-naked, waving his ceremonial sword at a tiny cat hiding behind the curtain. Field Marshal Lord Roberts, V.C., scourge of the Boers, broke out in a cold sweat if a cat walked past.

But Albert Schweitzer loved them so much that, though left-handed, he wrote out prescriptions with his right hand if a cat happened to be asleep on his other arm!

It has been said there is no single quality of the cat that man could not emulate to his advantage . . .

Were the medieval courts really on to something? Certainly cats *do* have healing powers. Their companionship has reduced the blood pressure of heart patients. Scientists in Ohio, found that if a criminally insane person kept a cat, his violent behaviour decreased dramatically.

Of the cat's prominent admirers, at least one, the 19th Century English writer, St George Mivart, actually dared place the cat higher than man at the summit of the animal kingdom.

When Merlin wandered in from the cold as a stray, he was willingly domesticating himself, but very much on his own terms. I hope I have been worthy of his affection. Certainly, like those ancient Egyptians at Bubastis, I have been adoring him ever since . . .

KING OF THE ANIMALS

'When I am playing with my cat, who knowes
whether she has more sport in dallying with me
than I have in gaming with her?'

Michel de Montaigne, *Essays*, 1580